Cryptocurrency

Enhancing Your Cryptocurrency Trading And Investment Achievements: Valuable Perspectives And Methodologies

(A Comprehensive Handbook For Novices On Generating Profits Through Cryptocurrency Investments)

Reginald Beaumont

TABLE OF CONTENT

What Is Cryptocurrency 1

Trading With Cryptocurrency 13

Ethereum 55

Cryptocurrency Trading Approaches Utilizing Technical Analysis 83

What Is The Reason For The Significant Fluctuations In Price? 107

Various Categories Of Cryptocurrencies 128

What Is Cryptocurrency

Cryptocurrencies, often referred to as cryptos, consist of decentralized peer-to-peer digital systems designed for monetary exchange. In this regard, it functions as legal tender that can be used for payment to any party willing to accept it in return for their merchandise or services. Furthermore, there is the option to convert it into an alternative cryptocurrency or a different form of currency referred to as fiat.

The term "cryptocurrency" is formed by combining two elements—a mathematical one and a financial one. Cryptology refers to the domain encompassing codes and ciphers that possess an exceptionally high degree of resistance against unauthorized access. It resembles the intricate plotlines and covert activities portrayed in espionage movies. However, the crux of the matter revolves around mathematics Certain mathematical concepts contribute to the complexity of cryptography as a scientific discipline. In its core, it pertains to the act of encoding data for transmission in a manner that renders it impervious to interception, tampering, or replication. It can be likened to a unique identifier or imprint that encapsulates the essence, meaning, or fundamental substance it conveys.

Cryptography manifests itself in various embodiments. When utilizing an internet-connected device that ensures secure communication, the transmitted message is enciphered, limiting access to the specific individuals involved in the transmission who possess the requisite decryption key to decipher the conveyed content. The encryption employs cryptographic measures to ensure this.

The subsequent segment of the period is comprised of currency. Currency has recently acquired the connotation of representing the fungible nature of the exchange medium. Consequently, you have the ability to trade it for any item or commodity of your choosing. One has the capacity to acquire an automobile at some future point, and the following day contribute to a charitable cause. Given its ubiquitous nature spanning nearly all aspects of human existence, currency emerges as the most optimal means to carry out transactions. While individuals continue to engage in the practice of bartering, wherein goods are exchanged for one another, they ultimately revert to utilizing currency to accurately assess the worth of such transactions. In addition to its practicality as a portable form of value stored on physical or digital mediums such as paper currency, debit cards, or credit cards, currency also functions as a medium of exchange for a wide range of goods and services, including but not limited to automobiles, bridges, and even delectable treats like ice cream.

When these components are combined, the result is a system that employs cryptographic techniques to encapsulate a transaction and assign it a numerical worth. Through encapsulation and assignment of a value, it can be extensively disseminated for consumption, thereby facilitating the process of selling or purchasing. However, during the implementation of this action, it has been discovered that the conventional currency model has proved inadequate due to the susceptibility of its value to governmental manipulation. The purchasing power that once enabled the acquisition of a complete ream of paper may potentially diminish to the extent of affording only half a ream in the future, owing to the deliberate expansion of currency supply by the governing authorities. One of the requisites we sought after was a mechanism that would prevent any sole entity from exerting control over global currencies in order to maintain stability solely through the unfettered interplay of market dynamics driven by supply and demand.

Currently, within the currency market, there exist measures involving arbitrary pegs and adjustments that are implemented with the aim of maintaining a particular currency at artificially predetermined levels. The monetary and fiscal policies of a single nation possess the potential to impact individuals residing on distant continents. The aforementioned drawback does not pertain to decentralized currencies that facilitate global business transactions. A digital currency, such as Bitcoin, is impervious to physical reproduction and cannot be subject to arbitrary expansion at the whim of any government.

This constitutes another characteristic of cryptocurrency, which has been devised in accordance with the principles and methodologies established by the unknown originators of Bitcoin. Its design ensures that the quantity in circulation remains fixed and cannot surpass a specified threshold.

Please take a moment to consider that. You possess a currency that will perpetually remain unaffected by any increments in the quantity of coins in circulation. The sole possibility that can occur to it is the fragmentation of its entirety into smaller fractions. In the event that 1 BTC is currently valued at $10,000, then it follows that 0.1 BTC would be worth $1000. This has two effects. The initial point to consider is that the value of BTC cannot be negatively influenced by the intentional injection of additional BTC, thus preventing any form of manipulation. The second point pertains to the eventuality of the BTC demand surpassing its supply. This would result in a continual increase in the valuation of BTC over time, accompanied by a gradual decrease in its fractional value.

For instance, hypothetically, we have the potential to divide 1 BTC into a thousand fractions, resulting in each fraction being valued at $10 in turn. This appears to closely resemble a stock split. And that precisely encapsulates the essence of the matter upon careful consideration. The price of the underlying asset can be adjusted to reflect the altered circumstances at that juncture. Presently, the most diminutive denomination, or unit, of Bitcoin ever exchanged consists of one hundred millionth of a BTC, equivalent to 0.00000001 BTC. At the prevailing exchange rate of $10,000, the amount translates to a value of .01 cents in equivalent U.S. dollars.

However, the advantage that you may experience ultimately dissipates as dividing the currency is tantamount to engaging in additional monetary issuance. It actually is not. The issuance of additional currency is a prerogative exercised by a governing authority. The valuation of BTC is entirely dictated by market forces. In the event that the market expands significantly, it becomes difficult to influence it unless there is a coordinated and comprehensive worldwide endeavor to exert influence upon it.

The combination of these factors renders cryptocurrencies, such as Bitcoin, ideal assets for speculative trading. The realm of speculative trading, encompassing both foreign exchange and cryptocurrencies, constitutes a symbiotic arrangement that is advantageous for the primary rationale we previously underscored. Speculative participants provide the market with essential liquidity, thereby establishing a stable foundation, while also furnishing transactional users with the necessary liquidity.

In the absence of a central governing body and legal enforcement, the lack of transactional security and the presence of inherent hazards are evident. However, such was the precise intention behind Satoshi's design of the currency. In the absence of intervention from regulatory bodies and central financial institutions, which often adhere to political influences, the Bitcoin market remains unaffected by short-term and myopic manipulation.

This raises inquiries regarding the maintenance of the necessary documentation. There is no requirement for trust, and naturally, the confidence ordinarily placed in public officials to act in accordance with what is just is typically upheld through legal measures. However, these consequences manifest subsequent to the commission of the crime, when it is already beyond remedy. Consequently, trust is not inherent to the Bitcoin system. On the contrary, the entire process is propelled by factual documentation. All transactional details, commencing from the initial block of BTC up until the most recent transaction completed a few minutes ago, have been meticulously retained.

Where is it preserved? Every instance in which a bitcoin is transferred is recorded on each individual node. A node refers to each individual computer that establishes a connection with the

BTC network. It adheres to the peer-to-peer paradigm. In the P2P system (the peer-to-peer system), everyone who is on the network or using the service forms part of the group. In this scenario, each individual node serves as a computer that is currently connected to the system. Each computer is equipped with a client that is subsequently activated, establishing a connection to the network and effectively transforming said computer into a node.

Furthermore, the said node possesses the capability to retain pertinent transaction data. Every single transaction that takes place results in a record being meticulously logged in every individual node of the ledger. Therefore, there does not exist a singular central repository of ledger information; instead, there exist numerous repositories distributed among millions of computers on a global scale. It is not feasible to proceed with the removal of this ledger, as it maintains a comprehensive account of all transactions, thus bestowing legitimacy upon every subsequent transaction. This is due to the fact that the record is impervious to forgery, unlike conventional currency. And it is not susceptible to being printed in order to dilute its value.

The crux of the cryptocurrency lies in the network nodes and the blockchain, which serves the purpose of maintaining the ledger. This can be expressed in a more formal tone as follows: "It is referred to as a distributed system, as opposed to a centralized system utilized by governments to store and manipulate value." Additionally, this poses a challenge for individuals engaged in currency speculation ascertaining an accurate assessment of the currency's intrinsic worth. It undeniably augments the multifaceted aspects of risk. The aforementioned risk is not present in the realm of cryptocurrencies.

"Thus, it is imperative to bear in mind the distinguishing attributes of the cryptocurrency ecosystem:

Individually minted coins that are not able to be produced

There is no centralized repository of the currency's transactions.

Distributed functionality

Market-driven

Can't be counterfeited

Easily transmittable

There exists no documentation regarding the transactions.

Prior to proceeding, it is of utmost importance to bear in mind that acquiring a comprehensive comprehension of the operational mechanisms of Bitcoin and its associated cryptocurrencies is an essential requirement for one to effectively acquire the necessary skills to engage in currency trading.

Trading With Cryptocurrency

One undeniable certainty in the realm of trading is that the notion of perfectly timing trades is a fallacy. Regardless of one's efforts to flawlessly execute buying and selling strategies, slippage is an inherent occurrence that must be anticipated at all times. It is impractical to purchase at the lowest possible price and sell at the highest possible price. Therefore, it is imperative not to commit the error of depleting your wealth by injecting a greater sum of capital than originally planned, with the hope of attaining substantial financial gains. There is no universally applicable principle governing trading practices; rather, individual traders employ their own unique methodologies, which may evolve in proficiency or decline with increased experience. This entire concept operates in a comparable fashion with Cryptocurrency trading as well.

Do not excessively dwell upon past unsuccessful trades; instead, release them from your mind and proceed forward with the assurance that you will endeavor not to replicate such missteps. Regarding the practice of trading, it is evident that hindsight offers perfect clarity. There is no value in contemplating the hypothetical scenario of what it could have been like had you purchased Bitcoins ten years ago and profited from it at present. While it is indeed accurate that this endeavor holds the potential for substantial returns amounting to millions, it must be emphasized that the current juncture remains opportune. Select the appropriate cryptocurrency and commence engaging in cryptocurrency trading.

Cryptocurrency Trading Strategy

Cryptocurrency Trading Strategy encompasses the process of establishing clear trading objectives, carefully selecting the appropriate cryptocurrency, ensuring reasonable profit projections, and comprehending various trading patterns in order to formulate a well-structured plan. Once one has a thorough understanding of the intended goals, the plan becomes intelligible, and the execution is flawless.

The preservation of the initial investment is the crucial element to be taken into account in the context of cryptocurrency trading. Evaluate your financial position thoroughly and establish a precise sum you intend to invest in cryptocurrency trading. Do not invest funds of which you lack the capacity to bear potential losses in the event of trading failure. The loss ought not to disrupt your present way of life or inflict a financial impact upon you. Maintain adherence to the initial investment allocation you had determined for cryptocurrency trading. Do not engage in the enlargement of the capital sum during the course of the operation; endeavor to preserve the current capital amount.

Do not fixate on the sole objective of 'generating profits' - prioritizing the recovery of the initial capital and preventing significant losses is of utmost importance. Allocate a capital range of 1% - 5% of the predetermined sum for trading purposes, while commencing with conservative investments. Ensure that you have a well-defined contingency plan in place to effectively respond to adverse market conditions. Prioritize developing a well-devised strategy for establishing the price level at which you will execute a loss reduction, referred to as the implementation of a stop-loss measure to safeguard the market viability of your investments. Please ensure that the trade position size remains below 25%. If the price exhibits the anticipated performance, then the profit target level is satisfactory.

Ensure efficient entry and exit into your selected trades by monitoring market liquidity and diligently adhering to data feeds, particularly if you engage in short-term trading. When engaging in short-selling with the intention of attaining expeditious profits, it is imperative to exercise discernment in selecting the appropriate cryptocurrency exchanges.

Instances of formulating a strategic approach

In order to establish your own trading strategy, it is imperative to possess a comprehensive understanding of your preferred method of 'buying and selling'. Will you be making regular purchases/sales or will you be waiting for an opportune moment? Although day trading may offer potential for profitability, it is advisable to exercise caution when applying this strategy to cryptocurrency investments.

It is advisable to adopt a conservative approach by refraining from making any changes or transactions. By maintaining the current position, the potential risk exposure can be minimized as time progresses. However, it is expected that you possess the necessary acumen to discern the underlying implications of the market fluctuations, and thus determine an opportune moment to disengage. For instance, instead of adhering to a traditional six-month holding period, it would be wise to selectively invest in alternative cryptocurrencies, aside from Bitcoin or Ethereum, that align with the present market trajectory, and subsequently unload those holdings after a three-month duration. As a nascent cryptocurrency, it is unpredictable when the market may experience significant fluctuations; therefore, it is advisable to minimize the duration of the holding period in such situations.

The decrease in economic performance resulting from unforeseen systemic issues must be examined with the objective of mitigating losses and divesting accordingly.

What level of advantage can be derived from acquiring knowledge in Cryptocurrency trading strategies?

Compared to Bitcoins, trading with altcoins can yield larger and more favorable profits due to their reduced susceptibility to public speculation and irrelevant rumors. The pricing of these alternative cryptocurrencies can also provide significant fluctuations benefiting traders, given the relatively smaller market capitalization compared to the well-known Bitcoin. When examining alternative cryptocurrencies, it becomes evident that each one possesses its own distinct purpose and objective, tailored to cater to specific sectors.

Indeed, it is a veritable fact that the level of risk amplifies when engaging with altcoins; however, on a parallel note, the potential rewards therein are substantial. Monero, ZCash, Dash, etc. There exist a limited number of alternative cryptocurrencies that have the potential to generate significant returns at an accelerated rate. Trading requires strategic decision-making and the ability to swiftly identify profitable stocks.

By demonstrating a comprehensive understanding of your cryptocurrency trading strategies and consistently monitoring market trends, you will experience an enhanced level of profitability. When it comes to the cryptocurrency market, it is essential to develop an appropriate plan and carefully select a trading strategy. "Allow us to examine a straightforward approach:

Rather than engaging in trading with a solitary cryptocurrency, it would be prudent to diversify one's portfolio by considering multiple digital coins, preferably no less than three.

- Evaluate your risk tolerance and, accordingly, distribute proportions of your market capital.

- It is important to note that alternative cryptocurrencies such as Ether and Litecoin, among others, should be taken into consideration. exhibit a higher degree of stability, while certain alternative cryptocurrencies like NEM and ripple demonstrate similar trends. may exhibit increased volatility.

Distributing 50% of the investment capital into Bitcoin, 30% into ether, 15% into Dash, and 5% into ZCash has the potential to yield favorable profits for a trader. This statement is a general 'quotation' devoid of specific context. One may consider adjusting the percentages in accordance with their financial capabilities and the market analysis conducted.

The trading strategy which yielded positive outcomes for one trader does not inevitably guarantee comparable results for another trader. Each strategy that is formulated should be predicated upon one's personal experiences and financial capacity. To fully capitalize on the advantages of digital currency, a comprehensive understanding of cryptocurrency's operational and technical intricacies is paramount. Stay updated on cryptocurrency developments through social media channels, engage in discussions on relevant forums, actively contribute by providing insightful comments on crypto blogs, and so forth.

Exploring Promising Trading Strategies to Consider!

For Bitcoin

Upon the acquisition of Bitcoin through a reputable exchange, it is possible to employ the 'market order' option to vend the Bitcoin at the most favorable market rate attainable. The cryptocurrency platform called 'Kraken' offers a 'market' feature that enables the activation of market orders, facilitating the acquisition of Bitcoin at the most competitive sell order price.

Please consider establishing a waiting period ranging from 3 to 6 months. During this period, it is advisable to retain the acquired Bitcoins for a minimum duration of 3 months. However, if a significant price surge occurs, it is acceptable to exchange the coins for fiat currencies. Conversely, should the price increase be relatively insignificant in relation to the purchase date, it would be prudent to extend the waiting period by an additional 3 months before considering selling. Monitor and document the biweekly price escalations while investigating potential causative factors for any subsequent decreases. By doing so, you can endeavor to forecast potential fluctuations in prices at the culmination of your designated waiting period.

Please remember to securely store your Bitcoin in a reputable hardware wallet or paper wallet.

For Ether

In regards to Ether, it is advisable to retain the altcoin over an extended period and refrain from engaging in short-term trading or hasty selling. This viewpoint will undoubtedly be further substantiated upon learning about a trading event in 2017, wherein an Ethereum trader swiftly accumulated a profit of $1,142,400. Allow us to thoroughly examine the incident and gain a comprehensive understanding of what transpired:

In June 2017, there was an unforeseen and sudden decline in the Ethereum market, with its value plummeting from $300 to $0.10 within a matter of seconds, only to subsequently recover to $300 within the following moments. Surprised?

- The following details outline the event: In the GDAX cryptocurrency exchange platform, the price of Ether experienced an abrupt decline, plummeting from $300 to $0.10, as a result of a trader's execution of a multimillion-dollar sell order.

This resulted in a state of disorder, causing computers to initiate automatic selling of Ether through price-triggered 'sell' orders (where traders can configure an automatic selling option for their coins when the price significantly decreases)."

As a result of this occurrence, a substantial number of traders incurred significant financial losses. Nevertheless, amidst this situation, one Ethereum trader demonstrated astuteness by employing an automated mechanism to execute a purchase order at the most minimal price point available.

During a period where the price of Ether plummeted to $0.10, he made a strategic move by instructing the system to purchase 3809 Ether, which turned out to be highly advantageous.

- Upon the resurgence of the price to $300, the Ethereum trader found themselves in possession of Ether valued at $1,142,700, signifying a remarkable return on investment of 300,000% in mere minutes.

It is imperative to conduct a comprehensive analysis of the market's previous trading patterns to safeguard against unforeseen financial setbacks. Given the distinct market positioning of the crypto token 'Ether', it would be advisable to retain the coin for a slightly extended duration prior to engaging in any trading activities.

7. The Prospects for Blockchain Technology and Cryptocurrencies in the Coming Years

There is extensive discussion surrounding cryptocurrencies, and you may be intrigued to know what lies at the heart of this discourse. Undoubtedly, the application of blockchain technology emerges as a promising solution. Nonetheless, individuals often contemplate the future prospects of these concepts, as they are hesitant to allocate substantial capital towards investments without a clear understanding of the potential outcomes.

In this chapter, we shall undertake a thorough examination of the prospective developments in blockchain technology and cryptocurrencies. It is imperative that you give your utmost attention to this chapter, as it will elucidate several concepts that may confront you in times to come.

Initially, blockchain gained recognition worldwide due to its association with cryptocurrencies. However, as cryptocurrencies were the initial application of blockchain technology, there is a common misconception that blockchain emerged solely because of cryptocurrencies.

The blockchain represents a versatile business solution with applications extending beyond the realm of digital currencies. This implies that in the event of cryptocurrencies becoming obsolete at present, blockchain technology will persist in offering uninterrupted transaction opportunities for businesses.

At present, investors are currently employing a combination of both ideals. Thus, it becomes imperative to contemplate their interplay and ascertain their future utility over the years ahead. Will there still be crypto coins in the future? Shall the credibility and validity of the blockchain remain intact in the future? There exists a considerable number of answers to the posed questions; nevertheless, within the confines of this chapter, we have restricted our range of responses to four potential scenarios for the foreseeable future.

8. The prospective trajectory of cryptocurrency and blockchain technologies

1. Bitcoin will experience a decline in significance.

Despite being the inaugural coin to gain widespread recognition, it is probable that Bitcoin will relinquish its preeminent position in the forthcoming years. A plethora of coins have already made their presence known, and numerous others will come into existence with enhanced technologies, potentially causing Bitcoin's relegation to a secondary position.

2. Blockchain technology will find application in various other sectors.

Additionally, the blockchain services will experience expansion, as an increasing number of enterprises recognize its profound implications and endeavor to participate in this groundbreaking technological advancement. Prepare yourself for the forthcoming integration of blockchain technology within the realms of healthcare, entertainment, finance, and governance. Blockchain technology will inevitably lead to substantial disruptions, yielding ultimately favorable outcomes.

3. Digital currencies are poised to supplant traditional fiat currencies.

Certain individuals who are enthusiastic about cryptocurrency strongly advocate for its inevitable emergence as a replacement for conventional currencies in the forthcoming years. Cryptocurrencies are steadily gaining traction in mainstream finance, thus, notwithstanding the varying perspectives of governments with regards to its regulation, they will continue to emerge as a viable substitute for traditional fiat currencies.

4. Cryptocurrencies are expected to endure for an extensive period of time.

Cryptocurrencies have established a permanent presence. Although these digital currencies are characterized by their volatility, they have exhibited considerable advancement thus far, and are poised to exert a durable influence in the long run. Prepare yourself for an influx of additional cryptocurrencies in the foreseeable future.

This chapter presents future forecasts. However, it is important to note that predictions are susceptible to alterations influenced by the forthcoming reality. Nevertheless, these concrete indicators serve as compelling evidence for the potential prominence of cryptocurrencies and blockchain within the realm of digital finance.

We have reached the culmination of an exceptional voyage, and within the concluding segment lies a significant message for you—one that holds the key to developing and maintaining a lucrative cryptocurrency portfolio.

Chapter 8: Strategies for Investing in Supply Chain Blockchains

This global health crisis has exposed significant deficiencies in worldwide supply chain logistics and has highlighted the alarming speed at which disruptions can occur when circumstances demand immediate action. We have observed not only deficiencies in fundamental resources such as PPE and medication, but also an excess of minor commodities that need to be disposed of or destroyed due to disrupted supply chains. This has accelerated the adoption of blockchain technology by both states and organizations in their supply chain operations. Although most of the blockchains employed by these entities consist of private networks, global supply chains have also leveraged public cryptocurrency blockchains for enhancement. Given the current state of a burgeoning buyer market, the focus will inevitably shift towards the realm of cryptocurrencies, thereby paving the way for groundbreaking ventures in the space of supply chain digital currencies such as VeChain, Waltonchain, and Hedera Hashgraph. This has the potential to substantially spur the adoption of cryptocurrency blockchains in global supply chains. Is it possible for these cryptocurrencies to reach unprecedented heights in the future? Taking into account all factors, let us examine the extent of the damage to these stockpile chains and explore how cryptocurrency can rectify the situation. Tissues were scarce during the initial stages of this pandemic, among various other items. The sudden surge in demand rendered Personal Protective Equipment (PPE), such as face masks, scarce and precious, akin to an overnight transformation, and even the availability of chemicals necessary for manufacturing test kits became exceptionally rare. Although some of these deficiencies resulted from insufficient production and occasional protectionism, it is fair to say that inefficient supply chains were equally or perhaps even more responsible. In the context of our highly interconnected global society, it is an infrequent occurrence for any product to be manufactured entirely on-site. Irrespective of the country where an item is being sold, there is a high probability that at least some of the raw materials used in its production were sourced from external origins. This suggests that a wide range of goods have been produced and distributed using numerous supply chains. As is anticipated, it can be inferred that the market for the supply chain is equally lucrative. Determining the precise value of the global supply chain industry presents a certain level of challenge, as it varies depending on how one chooses to define it. An illustrative example would be the global retail network management market, which currently holds a value of approximately 20 billion dollars with projections indicating a doubling of this value over the upcoming decade. On the other hand, the valuation of the entire supply chain market amounts to several trillions of dollars, and some analysts estimate that the valuation of the digital supply chain market similarly reaches trillions of dollars, at the very least. This is the market in which crypto projects such as VeChain, Waltonchain, and Hedera Hashgraph, among many others, have been endeavoring to penetrate.

to establish a solid groundwork for themselves, taking into account their varying levels of accomplishment. Due to the widespread recognition of deficiencies in stockpile chains by governments and institutions worldwide, there is a growing inclination to leverage blockchain technology to enhance the resilience of inventory chains. This approach not only aims to mitigate the economic repercussions of the pandemic but also seeks to optimize cost-efficiency. Nevertheless, in what precise manner can blockchain contribute to the enhancement of these supply chains? Taking into account all factors, according to the book titled "The Supply Chain Revolution" by Don Tapscott, it can be observed that a significant number of supply chains worldwide employ email, telephone, and fax for the purpose of monitoring the flow of labor and goods. As previously demonstrated, this unstable institution does not fare favorably when subjected to pressure. Despite the prevalence of shortages, certain nations like Canada have demonstrated that the inverse outcome is attainable. Despite the fact that numerous Canadians were simultaneously struggling to afford meals, Canadian ranchers had to dispose of a substantial quantity of potatoes and a considerable volume of milk. This is primarily due to the fact that these products need to be delivered to restaurants and supply chains could not adapt quickly enough in order to distribute these goods in an alternate manner before their expiration. Blockchain addresses these supply chain issues in multiple ways. Immediately, blockchain has the potential to greatly impact the transportation of fragile goods. You may have undoubtedly become aware of the emerging Pfizer antibody which exhibits considerable potential in combating the Covid-19 virus. It has likely come to your attention that optimal storage conditions, particularly constant refrigeration, are essential for maintaining the effectiveness of this vaccine during transit. Although Pfizer intends to utilize their proprietary transportation methods for the distribution of these vials, nations cannot have full assurance that the appropriate conditions have been maintained throughout the entire supply chain. A blockchain represents the primary advancement that holds the potential to establish impeccable supervision through a consistently transparent and immutable approach. Moreover, the implementation of blockchain technology would contribute to the reduction of food wastage and the prevention of foodborne illnesses, as it enables the seamless traceability of production all the way from farm to consumer. Additionally, blockchains have the potential to enhance exchange settlements within the realms of both retailers and providers. Blockchain has made significant strides in facilitating payment mechanisms. They enable the possibility of executing tasks such as creating a sophisticated agreement that will automatically compensate a supplier upon the fulfillment of specific conditions, such as delivery or successful completion of services requested by a retailer. This represents a significant advancement from the costly and laborious invoicing procedures employed by the majority of supply chains, which can occasionally take months to resolve payments. Furthermore, blockchains have the capacity to bring transparency to both consumers and producers. The ongoing global health crisis has catalyzed an increase in the proliferation of counterfeit goods. This could potentially serve as part of the rationale behind the recent adoption of blockchain technology by numerous luxury brands, in order to provide assurance to their customers that their investment capital is being utilized for the purchase of authentic goods. Moreover, it will also enable a retailer to promptly ascertain if they are running low on a particular product within their various locations and warehouses. Indeed, they could potentially verify whether the supplier is also failing and if there are any alternative blockchain options available; in such a case, it should be feasible to smoothly transition to another solution with minimal disruption. Altering the existing arrangement of names, contact numbers, and fax numbers is not congruent. In essence, the act of acknowledging access to the blockchain of another supply chain network is being referred to. But where do cryptocurrency blockchains fit into this picture? In recent months, there have been several occurrences where cryptocurrency blockchains have been employed to enhance the efficiency of supply chains. In September 2020, VeChain became a chamber member of the coalition in China focusing on animal welfare and food processing, thereby providing supply chain support to over 130 companies, including renowned brands such as McDonald's, Starbucks, and Walmart. In that particular month, it was disclosed that Hedera Hashgraph had collaborated with a supply chain enterprise and consortium to monitor wine production in southern Australia. In the month of October, please take note of this information. This brings me to the fourth solution/point/change.

flexibility. When a supply chain is supported by Tezos, the Swiss municipality utilizes it to distribute financial aid to its residents as part of their efforts in responding to the Covid situation. Furthermore, there have been numerous philanthropic initiatives organized by the cryptocurrency community to contribute to the ongoing battle against the pandemic. For example, you received donations from Binance's cryptocurrency initiative aimed at combating Covid-19, which has been diligently monitoring the distribution of acquired contributions. Several international foundations also extended their financial resources to accept contributions in the form of digital currencies throughout the year 2020. However, that is the extent of its progression. The adoption of blockchain technology in supply chain applications by cryptocurrency networks has been largely underwhelming, save for VeChain, which has experienced significant adoption mainly in China. What could be the underlying cause of such a circumstance? A news feature from the year 2020 presents us with an indication. In January, news emerged that ConsenSys, a consortium formed by major global agricultural entities, reached out to a cryptocurrency software company called agreement in order to provide assistance in constructing their blockchain network. ConsenSys has no intention of employing a cryptocurrency blockchain for its supply chain, regardless. Instead, ConsenSys will employ Quorum, a privately replicated version of Ethereum developed by JP Morgan in collaboration with ConsenSys. Privately-owned enterprises exhibit limited interest in embracing public and permissionless blockchains. Taking into account all factors, it is imperative for them to possess the ability to safeguard sensitive information from the public domain. They are also considerably hesitant to adopt cryptocurrency blockchains due to regulatory ambiguity. This is the evaluation provided by Dr. Robert Lerney, a blockchain technologist specializing in the clinical domain within the United Kingdom. It is undeniable that the increase in ransomware attacks involving cryptocurrency has had a detrimental impact, particularly targeting critical healthcare institutions and supply chains that cryptocurrency projects aim to serve. Specifically, prominent technology companies such as IBM, Microsoft, and Google currently provide various services to support global network organizations and consequently hold considerable influence in the industry. It is highly likely that they will strive to maintain their prevailing position, and in the event that cryptocurrency initiatives indeed gain traction, all these technology giants need to do is exhibit their clientele a fresh narrative regarding the latest ransomware attack. Due to VeChain, they merely need to emphasize the aforementioned security breach that occurred in December 2019. Although there appears to be growing adoption of cryptocurrencies in the financial sector, I am of the opinion that true integration of crypto in the realm of supply chains is still a long way off. In any case, there is one factor that has the potential to expedite the process. There exists a commonly held misperception that all blockchains are inherently decentralized. This is not an accurate representation of the situation, which is why you might occasionally encounter the term "distributed ledger technology" being used interchangeably with blockchain when discussing the advancements made by governments or organizations in this area. This is because the term "distributed record" is a more accurate description of the systems they actually possess. In the event that you had made a formal inquiry regarding JP Morgan's Quorum blockchain location, it is probable that they would demonstrate to you a physical establishment or conceivably even a dedicated facility housing multiple interconnected servers overseeing a comprehensive database. Although their blockchain exhibits a decentralized structure wherein the organization remains functional even if a single server fails, it remains evident that it is ultimately centralized. In stark contrast, consider a blockchain such as Bitcoin that possesses a vast multitude of miners and nodes dispersed worldwide. There is not only a lack of weak links, but there is also a complete absence of any individual component having secondary access to the entire system, which I am confident JP Morgan possesses in relation to its Quorum chain and its widespread utilization. What is the significance of this? Undoubtedly, the primary objective of blockchain is to achieve decentralization, thereby eliminating any potential weak points. However, it is important to note that the supply chain blockchains being developed by technology companies exhibit a high degree of centralization. Irrespective of whether they are employing multiple physical locations for storing their blockchain, I would confidently assert that they possess administrative keys to that chain and all the data transmitted through it. Production network organizations would be amenable to partnering with prominent technology conglomerates until such time that their integrated blockchains encounter technical malfunctions, experience operational disruptions, or are discovered to have surreptitiously exploited their data for nefarious intents. To effectively achieve true decentralization, it is imperative to implement monetary incentives that incentivize individuals to uphold the principles of a decentralized organization. Consequently, individuals are awarded digital currency as a reward for engaging in the mining process or operating a hub. On the same note, being inactive for an extended period or engaging in malicious activities can result in the reduction of one's stakes on multiple proof-of-work blockchains. What potential consequences do you anticipate for these prominent technology companies in the event of malevolent behavior or substantial disruptions in their blockchains? They will be the observers witnessing our ascent on the VeChain journey to success as numerous clients flock towards the cryptocurrency realm seeking our innovative solutions. However, there exists an alternative potential outcome to this contemplative exercise that is significantly less pleasant. The utilization of blockchain technology can yield positive or negative outcomes depending on the manner in which it is employed. It brings me great satisfaction to learn about the utilization of Bitcoin by individuals in countries such as Venezuela and Lebanon, who leverage this digital currency as a means to safeguard their wealth in the face of failed economic policies implemented by their respective governments. I cannot express parallel sentiments upon encountering literature pertaining to dictatorial regimes employing blockchain technology for enhanced surveillance of their citizenry. Evidently, there are considerable disparities among these scenarios, and it is imperative to address this misapplication of blockchain before concluding our discussion. I recently perused a captivating article authored by Coindesk. The author illustrates how supply chain blockchains can be employed to artificially inflate the price of certain services and goods in order to manipulate consumer behavior. Given that the implementation of such value control necessitates centralized control, it genuinely prompts me to ponder who will be tasked with delineating the specific purchasing behaviors to be altered and what mechanisms will govern that process. There is an indication that it will not be highly fair. That level of power and influence would be formidable for any individual or organization, and it directly contradicts the decentralized principles of cryptocurrency. The importance of adhering to principles such as decentralization, safeguarding, and personal ownership constitutes the rationale behind the lack of emergence of digital identities and COVID contact tracing applications in cryptocurrency projects. Alternatively, the compatibility between the degree of security and information ownership facilitated by a crypto-based identification system or subsequent application appears incongruent with the extent to which government authorities expect their citizens to provide data. Although rather disquieting, it is indeed a legitimate cause for concern. Experts worldwide are urging individuals to relinquish a certain degree of personal liberty, privacy, and autonomy, which many find reluctant to relinquish. It is being undertaken with the aim of combatting a global infection, which is commendable. However, as is the case with most matters, the optimal strategy likely lies within a balanced approach. Furthermore, a multitude of individuals are unaware of the exact location of said center.

ground is. One can be certain that among the numerous adverse consequences of this pandemic, one of the most egregious outcomes has been. The intensification of power concentration among both the populace at large and the private sector, alongside the unfortunate consequence that many of the challenges being tackled by these consolidated entities could be more effectively addressed through a decentralized approach supported by transparent economic incentives. Their integrated blockchain solutions will only further exacerbate the situation. The only remaining course of action is to present them with the alternative choice and demonstrate to others how it is executed. In summary, the present pandemic has undoubtedly revealed the profound flaws and obsolescence inherent in our current supply chains. Thankfully, the advent of blockchain technology has arrived to modernize the supply chain industry to align with the demands of the 21st century. Blockchain has the potential to offer various advantages to supply chains, including but not limited to optimizing the transportation of fragile merchandise deliveries between suppliers, facilitating the smoothness of the production process, and streamlining the creation of new inventory pathways. While there are still tremendous opportunities for wealth creation, prominent tech giants such as IBM, Microsoft, and Amazon seem to have firmly entrenched themselves within the supply chain industry at present. In contrast to antibodies, when working with

Retailers have limited opportunities to achieve meaningful stability at present, given the apparent scarcity of space for cryptocurrency operations. Moreover, the decentralized blockchains being constructed by prominent technology conglomerates appear to exhibit considerable vulnerability to various centralization risks, such as service disruptions, cyber attacks, and malicious activities. As institutions increasingly embrace cryptocurrencies and establish regulatory frameworks, it is plausible that specialized digital currency initiatives focusing on supply chain innovations could surpass these tech giants, given the vulnerabilities exposed in their blockchain platforms. Blockchain represents a formidable innovation that, if exploited without proper safeguards, can potentially be misused. As individuals enthusiastic about cryptocurrency, it is our responsibility to disseminate the profound notion of decentralization and to demonstrate to the global community how sincere and transparent financial incentives can be leveraged to construct the improved world that we constantly hear about.

Ethereum

The purpose of Ethereum is to integrate and enhance the principles of scripting, altcoins, and on-chain meta-protocols, enabling developers to create consensus-based applications with scalability, standardization, feature-completeness, ease of development, and interoperability, all simultaneously provided by these diverse paradigms. Ethereum achieves this objective by constructing a highly comprehensive foundational platform, notably a blockchain embedding a Turing-complete programming language. This unique feature enables individuals to craft smart contracts and decentralized applications, granting them the capability to establish their own autonomous regulations concerning ownership, transaction formats, and state transition functions. A minimalist rendition of Namecoin may be encapsulated in a concise pair of code lines, whereas supplementary frameworks such as currencies and reputation systems can be constructed within a modest timeframe of less than twenty units. Smart contracts, cryptographic enclosures that possess valuable content and solely grant access upon fulfillment of specific conditions, have the capability to be developed on our platform as well. These smart contracts offer significantly greater potential compared to the script capabilities of Bitcoin, due to their incorporation of Turing completeness, awareness of value, blockchain integration, and state management.

Ethereum Accounts

In the Ethereuм network, the constituent elements of the system are referred to as "accounts". An account is defined by a 20-byte address and state transitions occur as straightforward transfers of value and information between these accounts. An Ethereum account comprises four fields:

- The nonce serves as a mechanism to ensure that each transaction can only be processed once.

- The current ether balance of the account.

The contractual code, should it be in existence

- The account's storage, which is initially void.

Ether serves as the primary internal cryptofuel within the Ethereum network and is utilized for the remittance of transaction fees. Broadly speaking, there exist two distinct classifications of accounts: externally owned accounts, which are governed by private keys, and contract accounts, which are governed by their respective contract code. In the context of an externally owned account, sending messages can be accomplished by generating and authenticating a transaction. On the other hand, within a contract account, each time it receives a message, its code is activated to facilitate reading, writing to internal storage, sending additional messages, or generating contracts in response.

Communications and Financial Interactions

"Messages" within the Ethereum network bear resemblance to "transactions" in Bitcoin, albeit exhibiting three notable distinctions. Initially, it is worth noting that within the Ethereum network, a communicative unit referred to as an "Ethereum message" can arise from either an external individual or a contract. On the contrary, a Bitcoin transaction can exclusively originate from an external source. Furthermore, there is a specific provision for Ethereum messages to incorporate data. Ultimately, the individual receiving an Ethereum message possesses the ability to reciprocate with a response in the event that it pertains to a contractual account. This demonstrates that Ethereum messages encompass the notion of functions as well.

In Ethereum, the benign term "transaction" is employed to designate the authenticated data encapsulation that preserves a message intented for transmission from a third-party owned account. Transactions encompass the recipient of the communication, a distinctive signature denoting the entity accountable for initiating the transaction, the quantities of ether involved, and the pertinent information for transmission, alongside two designated variables known as STARTGAS and GASPRICE. In order to mitigate the risks of exponential blow-up and infinite loops in the code, it is mandatory for each transaction to establish a predetermined threshold for the maximum number of computational steps of code execution allowed. This limit encompasses both the original message and any subsequent messages generated during the execution process. Commencing gas allocation is defined by the STARTGAS limit, while the GASPRICE denotes the remuneration imposed on the miner for each computational step performed. If the execution of a transaction is terminated due to gas depletion, all changes made to the state are rolled back, except for the payment of fees. If the transaction execution comes to a halt with some gas remaining, the remaining portion of the fees is returned to the sender. Furthermore, there exists a distinct category of transaction, accompanied by an associated message type, designated to initiate the creation of a contractual arrangement. Notably, the address of a contract is determined through the computation of the hash value derived from the account nonce and transaction data.

One significant outcome of the message mechanism is the inherent principle of Ethereum known as the "first-class citizen" property. This concept pertains to the equal capabilities of contracts in comparison to external accounts, enabling them to perform actions such as message transmission and the creation of additional contracts. This allows contracts to simultaneously fulfill multiple roles. For instance, a member of a decentralized organization can act as an escrow account between a cautious individual utilizing customized quantum-proof Lamport signatures and a co-signing entity incorporating a five-key security system. The main advantage of the Ethereum platform lies in the fact that the decentralized organization and escrow contract do not have any concerns regarding the type of account held by each party involved in the agreement.

The state transition function for Ethereum, denoted as APPLY(S,TX) -> S', can be specified as follows:

1. Verify the adequacy of the transaction, namely, Ensuring that the signature is valid and the nonce matches that of the sender's account, while also confirming

the proper number of values are present. If not, then an error should be returned.

2. Derive the transaction fee by multiplying STARTGAS with GASPRICE, and ascertain the sender's address based on the signature. Deduct the fee from the balance in the sender's account and increase the sender's nonce. In the event that an insufficient balance exists to complete the transaction, an error should be returned.

3. Establish the value of GAS as STARTGAS, and deduct a specified amount of gas per byte to cover the bytes involved in the transaction.

4. Execute the transfer of funds from the sender's account to the receiving account. In the event that the designated recipient account has not yet been established, it should be created. If the account receiving the transaction is a contract, execute the contract's code either until it reaches completion or until the execution exhausts its gas limit.

5. In the event that the value transfer is unsuccessful due to insufficient funds on the part of the sender, or if the code execution exhausts the available gas, it is necessary to undo all state changes except for the payment of fees, and subsequently assign the fees to the miner's account.

6. Alternatively, kindly proceed with reimbursements of the remaining gas fees to the sender and ensure that the fees incurred for gas consumption are appropriately allocated to the miner.

As an illustration, consider the scenario where the code within the contract is:

if !contract.storage[msg.data[0]]:

The value of 'msg.data[1]' is assigned to the key 'msg.data[0]' in the contract's storage.

Please be advised that the contract code is actually composed in the low-level EVM code. The aforementioned illustration, however, has been presented in Serpent, our high-level language, for the purpose of clarity. It is important to note that it is fully capable of being compiled into EVM code. Assuming that the storage of the contract is initially empty, let us consider a scenario in which a transaction is sent with a value of 10 ether, 2000 gas, a gas price of 0.001 ether, and two data fields: [2, 'CHARLIE']. The procedure for determining the state transition function in this scenario is as outlined below:

1. Please verify the transaction to ensure its validity and proper formatting.

2. Please verify that the sender of the transaction possesses a minimum of 2 ether, which can be calculated as 2000 multiplied by 0.001. If that is the case, then deduct 2 ether from the sender's account.

3. Set the initial gas value to 2000; under the assumption that the transaction consists of 170 bytes and the fee for each byte is 5, deduct 850 in order to retain a remaining gas of 1150.

4. Deduct an additional 10 units of ether from the sender's account and transfer it to the account associated with the contract.

5. Run the code. In this particular scenario, the process is straightforward: it verifies whether the storage at index 2 of the contract is being utilized, observes that it is not in use, and subsequently assigns the value CHARLIE to the storage at index 2. Assuming that 187 units of gas are consumed, the remaining quantity of gas would be 963 units, calculated as 1150 minus 187.

6. Remit the value of 963 multiplied by 0.001, which amounts to 0.963 ether, back to the sender's account, and restore the resultant state.

In the absence of a contract at the receiving end of the transaction, the total transaction fee would be determined by the multiplication of the provided GASPRICE and the length of the transaction in bytes. The data sent alongside the transaction would be inconsequential. Furthermore, it should be observed that messages initiated through contracts have the ability to allocate a specific limit to the computational processes they generate. In the event that the subsidiary computation exhausts its allocated gas, it will be reversed only up until the point of the initial message invocation. Therefore, similar to transactions, contracts can effectively conserve their limited computational resources by establishing stringent limits on the sub-computations they generate.

Code Execution

The programming language used in Ethereum contracts is composed of low-level, stack-based bytecode referred to as "Ethereum Virtual Machine code" or "EVM code." The code is comprised of a sequence of bytes, with each byte corresponding to an operation. Code execution, in general, involves an ongoing iteration whereby the operation at the current program counter - which initially starts at zero - is repeatedly performed, followed by incrementing the program counter by one, until the completion of the code is reached or an error, STOP, or RETURN instruction is detected. The operations have the ability to store data in three different types of space.

• The stack is a container that follows the last-in-first-out principle, allowing the pushing and popping of 32-byte values.

• Memory, a byte array with limitless scalability

The agreement entails the utilization of a long-term storage facility within the contract, serving as a key-value store specifically designed to accommodate keys and values, each comprised of 32 bytes. Contrary to stack and memory, which reset once computation concludes, storage endures in the long term.

The code has the capability to retrieve the value, sender, and data of the incoming message, along with the block header data. Moreover, the code is capable of providing a byte array of data as an output.

The execution model of Earned Value Management (EVM) code in a formal context is unexpectedly straightforward. While the Ethereum virtual machine is operational, its complete computational state can be accurately described by the tuple (block_state, transaction, message, code, memory, stack, pc, gas). In this context, block_state refers to the global state encompassing all accounts and includes information such as balances and storage. During each iteration of execution, the current instruction is determined by extracting the byte specified by the program counter, and each instruction has its own definition in terms of its impact on the tuple. For instance, the ADD operation retrieves and combines two elements from the stack, calculates their sum, decrements the gas by 1, increments the program counter (pc) by 1, while the SSTORE operation removes the top two elements from the stack and inserts the second element into the contract's storage at the index specified by the first element. This operation also reduces gas by a maximum of 200 and increments the pc by 1. Although there exist numerous methods to optimize the performance of Ethereum through just-in-time compilation, it is possible to achieve a fundamental implementation of Ethereum with a concise codebase consisting of a few hundred lines.

Blockchain and Minning

The Ethereum blockchain bears resemblance to the Bitcoin blockchain in several aspects, albeit it does exhibit certain distinctions. The fundamental distinction between Ethereum and Bitcoin in terms of their blockchain architecture lies in the fact that, unlike Bitcoin, Ethereum blocks incorporate both the transaction list and the latest state.

In addition to that, two other values, namely the block number and the difficulty, are also stored within the block. The block validation algorithm in Ethereum can be described as follows:

1. Verify the existence and validity of the preceding block.

2. Please verify that the timestamp of the block is larger than the timestamp of the referenced previous block and smaller than 15 minutes into the future.

3. Verify the validity of the block number, difficulty, transaction root, uncle root, and gas limit, which are various low-level Ethereum-specific concepts.

4. Please verify the validity of the evidence provided for the task on the block.

5. Let S[0] denote the STATE_ROOT of the previous block.

6. Let TX represent the block's transaction list, comprising n transactions. For every element in the

range from 0 to n-1, assign the value of APPLY(S[i], TX[i]) to S[i+1]. In the event that any applications encounter an error, or if the cumulative gas consumption within the block surpasses the GASLIMIT, the appropriate response would be to issue an error.

7. Designate S_FINAL as S[n], taking into account the block reward disbursed to the miner.

8. Verify whether S_FINAL is equivalent to the STATE_ROOT. If the aforementioned condition is met, the block shall be deemed valid; conversely, if the condition is not met, it shall be considered invalid.

The proposed methodology may initially appear highly inefficient due to the necessity of storing the complete state alongside each block. However, it should be noted that its efficiency should be comparable to that of Bitcoin. The rationale behind this is that the state is stored within the tree structure, and subsequent modifications to the tree only affect a small portion after each block. Therefore, in most cases when comparing two contiguous blocks, the majority of the tree should have identical characteristics, thus allowing for the storage of data once and its subsequent referencing through pointers (i.e., hashes of subtrees). A specific variety of tree, referred to as a "Patricia tree," is employed in order to achieve this outcome. This entails a modification to the concept of the Merkle tree, which enables the seamless insertion and deletion of nodes, rather than solely allowing for modifications, thereby ensuring efficiency. Furthermore, due to the fact that all the state information is encompassed within the final block, there is no necessity to retain the complete historical record of the blockchain. This approach, if implemented in Bitcoin, has the potential to yield space savings ranging from 5 to 20 times the current storage requirements.

Applications

By and large, there exist three categories of applications atop the Ethereum platform. The initial classification pertains to financial applications that equip users with enhanced capabilities for effectively managing and engaging in contractual agreements utilizing their monetary resources. This encompasses sub-currencies, financial derivatives, hedging agreements, savings accounts, testamentary documents, and ultimately, certain categories of comprehensive employment contracts. The subsequent class pertains to applications with a partially financial nature, wherein monetary transactions occur alongside a significant non-monetary aspect in the activities performed. An exemplary instance in this category would be the implementation of self-regulating rewards for resolving computational problems. In conclusion, there exist certain applications, such as online voting and decentralized governance, that do not possess any financial characteristics.

Token Systems

Blockchain-based token systems have a wide array of applications, extending from sub-currencies that represent assets such as USD or gold, to stocks issued by companies, individual tokens that represent smart property, and even token systems that have no connection to conventional value but are utilized as point systems for incentivization.

Implementing token systems in Ethereum can be remarkably straightforward. The crux of the matter lies in recognizing that every currency or token system essentially functions as a database with a singular operation: the deduction of X units from A and the transfer of X units to B, under the condition that (i) X possesses at least X units prior to the transaction, and (ii) the transaction receives approval from A. Incorporating this logic into a contract is the sole requirement for the implementation of a token system.

The fundamental code required to implement a token system in Serpent can be represented as:

Originating from the sender

Assign the value of msd.data[0] to the variable 'to'.

The value is equal to the second element of the message data.

If the value is less than or equal to the contract storage amount:

The variable "contract.storage[from]" is reduced by the value stored in "contract.storage[from]".

The value assigned to contract.storage[to] is equal to contract.storage[to].

This represents a direct implementation of the state transition function for the banking system as described previously in this document. To facilitate the initial step of distributing the currency units and address any potential edge cases, it is necessary to incorporate a few additional lines of code. Ideally, a function would be included to enable other contracts to inquire about the balance of a specific address. However, that encompasses the entirety of the matter. In theory, it is possible for Ethereum-based token systems to incorporate an additional crucial aspect that on-chain Bitcoin-based meta-currencies lack: the capability to directly settle transaction fees using that particular currency. The manner in which this would be implemented involves maintaining an ethereum balance within the contract, which would be utilized to reimburse the sender for any ethereum used to cover fees. Additionally, this balance would be replenished by collecting the internal currency units obtained from fees and subsequently reselling them through a continuous running auction. Therefore, individuals would be required to "initiate" the activation process for their accounts using either, but once the either is present, it would be capable of being used again because the contract would reimburse it on every occasion.

Financial derivatives and Stable-Value Currencies" can be restated in a more formal tone as: "Financial instruments derived from monetary contracts and Currency instruments designed to maintain a stable value

Financial derivatives represent the predominant utilization of a 'smart contract', and are among the most straightforward to execute in code. The primary obstacle in implementing financial contracts lies in the fact that most of them necessitate referencing an external price ticker. For instance, a highly desirable application involves a smart contract that mitigates the volatility of ether (or another cryptocurrency) in relation to the US dollar. However, accomplishing this requires the contract to possess knowledge of the current ETH/USD valuation. The most straightforward method to accomplish this task is by means of a "data feed" agreement administered by a designated party (such as). The NASDAQ is structured in a manner that enables one party to make necessary modifications to the contract, while also facilitating an interface that allows other contracts to send a message to the said contract and receive a response containing the relevant price information.

Considering the crucial element, the hedging contract would appear as follows.

1. Kindly await the submission of 1000 ether by party A.

2. Please await the input of 1000 ether by party B.

3. Store the USD value of 1000 ether, obtained through querying the data feed

contract, within the storage mechanism, denoting this as $x.

4. After the expiration of a 30-day period, it is permissible for either party A or party B to initiate a contractual communication in order to transfer an amount equivalent to $x worth of ether, as determined by querying the data feed contract for the updated price, with party A receiving the specified amount and the remainder being allocated to party B.

This particular agreement holds immense potential within the realm of cryptocurrency-based commerce. One of the primary concerns raised regarding cryptocurrency is its volatility. While numerous users and merchants may desire the security and convenience offered by dealing with cryptographic assets, they may be unwilling to confront the possibility of experiencing a 23%

loss in the value of their funds within a single day. Until this point in time, the most commonly proposed solution has been the utilization of issuer-backed assets. The concept involves an issuer creating a sub-currency wherein they retain the authority to issue and revoke units. They would then offer one unit of the currency to anyone who presents them with one unit of a specified underlying asset, offline for instance. gold, USD). The entity further pledges to deliver a single unit of the underlying asset to individuals who return one unit of the crypto-asset. This mechanism facilitates the conversion of any non-cryptographic asset into a cryptographic asset, under the condition that the issuer can be deemed trustworthy.

In practical application, it must be acknowledged that not all entities can be relied upon with certainty, and there are instances where the banking system lacks the necessary strength or displays unwelcoming behavior, thereby preventing the viability of such services. Financial derivatives offer an alternative. In this case, rather than a sole entity supplying the necessary funds to support an asset, a decentralized marketplace comprising of speculators who believe that the value of a cryptographic reference asset will increase assumes that function. Unlike issuers, speculators do not have the option to default on their side of the agreement due to the fact that the funds are held in escrow by the hedging contract. Please take note that this approach is not entirely decentralized as it still relies on a trusted source to supply the price ticker. However, it can be argued that even with this dependency, it represents a significant improvement in terms of reducing the need for infrastructure (unlike being an issuer, providing a price feed does not require licenses and can likely be categorized as free speech) and mitigating the potential for fraudulent activities.

Cryptocurrency Trading Approaches Utilizing Technical Analysis

Fibonacci Retracements

These are the renowned instruments that traders employ for detecting the inflection points in cryptocurrency prices. Absence of assistance from this tool may result in traders becoming trapped in unreliable bitcoin transactions, potentially resulting in avoidable financial losses.

Although the primary application of the Fibonacci retracement tool is in conventional stock or forex markets, it is worth noting that this tool can yield remarkable results in the realm of cryptocurrency markets as well.

Within this comprehensive guide, we shall delve into the intricate technical characteristics of this tool. Ultimately, you will acquire the knowledge to effectively utilize it for identifying crucial levels within a trading chart.

Could you provide an explanation of the concept known as Fibonacci retracement levels?

The Fibonacci Retracement Level is a tool that identifies concealed levels of horizontal lines of resistance and support. These levels indicate potential points at which bitcoin prices may undergo a reversal. The fundamental Fibonacci levels encompass percentages of 23.6%, 38.2%, 61.8%, and 78.6%.

The Fibonacci retracement is an extrapolation derived from the Fibonacci sequence, which is commonly observed in various natural phenomena and extensively utilized in mathematical calculations. It was a mathematician of Italian origin who initially made the discovery. They are employed by financial traders to analyze price charts with the objective of identifying potential inflection points.

What is the significance of the ratio?

The concept of Fibonacci retracement entails the utilization of a percentage to assess the impact on the preceding trend. Retestation offers an indication of the extent to which the preceding trend is anticipated to be rectified prior to the resumption of the former trend. The Fibonacci tool facilitates the identification of market trends by converting percentage values into bitcoin price levels.

Reversal can commence from four primary levels of return.

23.6%

38.2%

61.8%

78.6%

This particular Fibonacci ratio may appear to be arbitrary information, but it is not. Their origins can be traced back to the ancient series of organic numbers unearthed by humanity seven centuries ago.

Who Created Fibonacci Retracement?

The Fibonacci retracement percentage was established through the ordering and arrangement of Fibonacci numbers. Leonardo da Pisa is credited with the discovery and dissemination of the numerical sequence outlined in the publication known as Liber Abaci, also known as The Book of Numbers, released in the year 1202.

The sequence of numbers derived from the Fibonacci series takes on the following pattern:

The sequence presented is a series of numbers that follows the Fibonacci sequence.

The subsequent value in the sequence consistently amalgamates the preceding two values. The Fibonacci number can be determined by examining the neighboring numbers within the sequence.

Fibonacci number sequence

As an illustrative instance, the division of 21 by 34.6176 is undertaken. Take note of the manner in which the ratio between two successive numbers tends towards .618 as the sequence of numbers expands towards the right. The proportion of .618 corresponds to a value of 61.8%, which is considered one of the significant levels.

We have the option to reapply this method by dividing the sequence with each subsequent number.

The second retracement number in the Fibonacci sequence is to be divided by 55.

2nd number

In the subsequent illustration, the mathematical operation entails the division of 21 by 55. The numerical relationship between two consecutive terms in the sequence undergoes a transformation from 0.382, equivalent to 38.2% when expressed in percentage form, to the subsequent pivotal level.

3rd number

When employing this approach of dividing each of the third numerals within the sequence, the outcome obtained is the quotient derived from dividing 21 by 89. 2360. The ratio experiences an increase to .236, equivalent to 23.6% when the numerical sequence is shifted from left to right. This aligns with the third numeral in the Fibonacci retracement sequence.

The fourth and ultimate level can be expressed as 78.6% or .786, which is equivalent to the square root of .618, the initial pivotal level.

Computation of Fibonacci Retracement Ratio

In order to effectively utilize this tool, it is imperative that we possess a comprehensive understanding of the prevailing trend. The methodology of Fibonacci retracement involves quantifying the extent of the trend before subdividing it into four pivotal levels.

Price trend

In the given illustration, let us consider the commencement of an upward trend at $250, culminating at $350, resulting in a gain of 100.

The four ratios of 23.6%, 38.2%, 61.8%, and 78.6% are indicative of the trend size, which has a value of $100.

Determine the Fibonacci Retracement ratio

The initial retracement level, situated at 23.6%, will result in a correction that surpasses the higher price by 23.60.

A deduction of $23.60 from $350 yields a sum of $326.40.

The second retracement level, which stands at 38.2%, intends to rectify a value of exactly 38.20 units from the $350 peak (derived from the 100-unit upward trend multiplied by 38.2%, resulting in $38.20).

The computations remain consistent for the third and fourth levels, employing multiplication factors of 61.8% and 78.6% respectively.

Upon conducting these calculations, we have identified four distinct price zones at which the potential correction in the downward trend may cease, and subsequently initiate a reversal in the upward trajectory. The price comes to a temporary halt at 38.2% before subsequently declining to 61.8% in the provided illustration. Over time, prices exhibit a tendency to reach a state of stability and revert back to the 38.2% zone.

Luckily, contemporary charting packages possess the ability to automatically tally these computations and depict the horizontal price range on the chart. Therefore, your task simply entails acquiring the necessary proficiency in utilizing the Fibonacci retracement tool.

How to Create Fibonacci Retracement Levels

The utilization of tools greatly facilitates the process of delineating Fibonacci retracement levels.

To ascertain the presence of upward and downward price movements, in order to delineate Fibonacci retracement lines.

Initially, ascertain a comprehensive trend to which you intend to apply the principles of Fibonacci retracement.

Discover a charting instrument referred to as "Fibonacci retracement," which can be found on various charting software platforms, including Trading View.

Upon initiating the tool, commence by selecting the outset of the trend

The second click occurs upon reaching the conclusion of the entire trend.

Adjust the observable increments to reflect percentages of 23.6, 38.2, 61.8, and 78.6.

At this juncture, the chart will display the Fibonacci retracement levels. Traders will engage in transactions based on these levels in order to ascertain potential reversal points within subsequent corrections.

Employ the Fibonacci Retracement tool for the purpose of conducting cryptocurrency trading.

The application of the Fibonacci retracement tool proves to be highly user-friendly and advantageous to employ during cryptocurrency trading endeavors.

Initial Step: Initially, identify a comprehensive trend. The tool is applicable to both upward and downward trends. This tool can be utilized across various time frames depicted on the chart as well.

Proceed to Step 2: Following that, proceed to draw Fibonacci retracement lines in the direction of the concluded trend. This entails the act of drawing the Fibonacci retracement tool from the left to the right to encompass an entire upward trend. To achieve a comprehensive decline, slide the pattern horizontally from left to right, making a brief halt at the termination of the downward trend.

Step 3: Anticipating a decline in price within the vicinity of the four pivotal levels. Take note of these crucial levels in order to gauge the potential price reversal.

Step 4: Adhering to the trajectory of the initial trend when initiating the trade. The resurgence of the ascending pattern indicates a forthcoming decrease in prices. Subsequently, it is advisable to execute a swift trade in proximity to any of the four crucial Fibonacci retracement levels. Certain traders may choose to enter the return position while disregarding any potential risks. Other analysts will ascertain the price's response and await further indications of significant escalation before embarking on a long-term position.

Risk management techniques

Once a favorable trading prospect has been identified, it is imperative for traders to ensure that the stop loss is placed below the swing of the long trade or just above the swing high of the short setup. Establish a robust risk-to-reward ratio by aiming for a minimum of twice the amount of the stop loss.

The Fibonacci retracement tool exhibits its highest efficacy when employed in conjunction with indicators of technical analysis. For instance, the utilization of Fibonacci levels can generate both buying and selling indications, however, it remains uncertain whether the market will subsequently reverse its direction. It is advisable to verify through the use of technical indicators such as Bollinger Bands, Stochastic RSI, or the Ichimoku Cloud.

Illustration of Fibonacci retracement applied to the price movement of bitcoin

There exist a multitude of instances wherein the prices of bitcoin have exhibited fluctuations in close proximity to Fibonacci retracement levels. The market exhibits a high degree of dynamism, thereby enabling the observation of these instances across diverse chart time frames.

An illustration of Bitcoin trading utilizing the Fibonacci retracement technique.

Subsequent to registering a decline on November 26, 2020, Bitcoin exhibited an approximately 23% increase, thus concluding a pattern as observed on the 1-hour chart. When the tool is implemented from point A to point B, it gives rise to these areas of significance on the chart.

According to the chart data, it can be observed that the bitcoin exhibits signs of increasing momentum upon reaching the retracement threshold of 23.6%. Subsequently, the bitcoin attains a 38.2% threshold during the subsequent period of correction on three distinct occasions (indicated in blue).

The value of bitcoin eventually dips beneath the 38.2% retracement level and subsequently locates a new level of support in the vicinity of the 61.8% retracement level. The price subsequently oscillates two times within the range of the 61.8% and 38.2% Fibonacci retracement levels (as indicated by the highlights marked in orange).

The values of bitcoin are currently experiencing an upward trajectory, surpassing both the .382 and .236 levels after establishing support at a retracement level of 61.8%. Please be aware that once the 23.6% level is surpassed, Bitcoin exhibits trading activity above this level (indicating a strong positive signal) prior to attaining new record-breaking highs.

When the prices of Bitcoin surpass the Fibonacci retracement level in a direct manner, it may suggest that the market is poised for an upward movement. A trader will endeavor to take a prolonged pause when the market surpasses the subsequent Fibonacci level, while implementing a stop-loss order slightly lower than the present swing low. Strive to achieve a minimum of twice the distance as your stop loss.

Bitcoin Trading Example

"Fibonacci retracement in Bitcoin trading:

In September 2020, Bitcoin initiated a fresh bullish trend. This upward trajectory came to a halt and abated in April 2021. The price of Bitcoin commenced a corrective phase.

The value of bitcoin was bolstered at the 38.2% retracement level on two distinct instances. Frequently, one would observe an increase in prices when transitioning from one Fibonacci retracement level to the next. In the aforementioned diagram, it can be observed that Bitcoin has exhibited a recurring pattern of fluctuating between the thresholds of 38.2% and 23.6%, symbolizing the ongoing struggle between bullish and bearish market forces. This exemplification serves to demonstrate the significance that Fibonacci retracement levels, both for upward and downward movements, hold within the market.

Verifying the accuracy of Fibonacci using additional technical indicators.

The utilization of a Fibonacci retracement proves to be a highly effective and valuable tool. Nevertheless, traders typically incorporate additional tools to enhance the reliability of their signals.

Fibonacci extensions are a inherent counterpart to retracement tools. This tool possesses the capabilities to ascertain the potential extent of the present trend.

Candlestick formations and trend lines are employed in tandem with Fibonacci retracement levels. In the event that the bitcoin approaches the retest level, it would be advisable to observe a candlestick pattern as a means of substantiating the continuation of the upward trend, such as the occurrence of a bullish wrap.

Ultimately, the Elliott Wave Theory extensively employs Fibonacci retracements. The methodology employed to examine the market's geometric characteristics is referred to as Elliott Wave analysis.

Boundaries

Fibonacci retracements represent efficacious methodologies; however, their interpretation can easily be misconstrued.

Initially, in the event that a trader renders them with imprecision, it may result in the depiction of inaccurate levels on the chart.

Additionally, smaller cryptocurrency markets may exhibit lower trading volumes compared to major market capitalizations, such as bitcoins. Consequently, the indications provided by Fibonacci retracement in a minor market are deemed to be untrustworthy.

Ultimately, given the availability of 4 distinct levels, the trader may inadvertently direct attention to an incorrect level, thereby risking the loss of a profitable trade or the acceptance of an unprofitable one.

What is Blockchain?

Blockchain represents an ingenious breakthrough advanced by an undisclosed collective or individual, operating under the alias Satoshi Nakamoto. Blockchain technology is widely regarded as the fundamental infrastructure of the emerging digital landscape. Blockchain serves as a comprehensive, publicly accessible ledger for each and every Bitcoin transaction, wherein miners meticulously document the solved block accomplished through algorithmic computations. Cryptocurrencies are protected by encryption mechanisms that require the resolution of complex mathematical problems to facilitate any transaction.

First and foremost, blockchain meticulously verifies each transaction, and this ledger is impervious to modification by any individual. When it pertains to monetary matters, individuals are obligated to place their trust in a third party in order to successfully carry out a transaction. However, with the advent of cryptocurrency, the conventional reliance on intermediaries has been replaced. The utilization of blockchain technology has facilitated the elimination of intermediaries in all online transactions that you engage in. By employing mathematical algorithms and cryptography, blockchain facilitates the creation of an openly accessible and decentralized database that records all transactions involving value. The potential applications of blockchain technology are limitless, and the presence of third-party organizations may no longer be deemed essential.

Similar to other technological advancements, cryptocurrencies also have their drawbacks. However, as long as they yield favorable outcomes and enhance the daily productivity and efficiency of individuals, they will inevitably remain an integral component of the beneficial technologies that enhance the lives of people. Prior to engaging in online mining ventures and currency investments, it is advisable to conduct thorough preliminary research to acquire a comprehensive understanding of the underlying mechanics and evaluate the associated risks associated with investing in such ventures. In contemporary times, a growing number of individuals are actively seizing every available opportunity to minimize their expenses and maximize their financial returns through the most convenient and effortless means. However, it is important to bear in mind that every advancement does not always progress seamlessly. There will undoubtedly be numerous challenges and obstacles encountered along the path to making such enhancements. Similar to the current volatility observed in digital currencies such as Bitcoin, it is uncertain whether potential remedies can be discovered by innovators in the foreseeable future to address this inherent drawback of cryptocurrencies. The individual or individuals responsible for the creation of this cryptocurrency deserve gratitude as they have effectively resolved the double spending concerns for the foreseeable future.

What Is The Reason For The Significant Fluctuations In Price?

Upon embarking on your venture into cryptocurrency investment, you will undoubtedly discern that it stands as one of the most capricious and dynamic assets within the realm of the investment market. As previously indicated, the price of the item can experience significant fluctuations amounting to thousands of dollars on a daily basis. Within this chapter, we shall elucidate the rationale behind this phenomenon and offer guidance on appropriate courses of action.

Cryptocurrency in comparison to traditional fiat currency
The most effective approach to comprehending cryptocurrencies is through a comparative analysis with traditional forms of currency, commonly referred to as fiat currencies. Fiat currencies, alternatively known as

traditional forms of legal tender, serve as the universally accepted medium of exchange within a given nation. In the context of the United States, the official currency in use is the US Dollar, whereas Mexico employs the Mexican Peso and Canada adopts the Canadian Dollar.

These fiat currencies primarily comprise physical currency notes and coins, as well as virtual representations manifested as digital data on electronic devices. Nevertheless, they are regarded with esteem as an instrument for facilitating the exchange of commodities and resources due to a multitude of factors. The primary reason is that all individuals within a specific jurisdiction concur with both the worth and legality of the said matter.

The second rationale for the widespread acceptance of fiat currencies lies in their inherent stability of value. If one comes across a recently manufactured car, the value of which is estimated to be $20,000 presently, there is a high probability that it will maintain this price point up until tomorrow. As a matter of fact, all businesses possess the prerogative to establish any desired price for their products or services. Women's handbags, for instance, can range in value from a few dollars to several thousand dollars. However, business owners and managers face constraints imposed by market dynamics, necessitating them to make pricing choices based on rational considerations. As a consequence of this, the majority of the goods available in the market are priced relatively equitably, taking into account the prevailing dynamics of supply and demand.

One of the contributing factors to the stability of fiat currencies lies in their management by the central bank of a nation. In the United States, we have the Federal Reserve System overseeing the utilization and exchange of the US currency. Every nation possesses its own iteration of a central bank.

The central bank consistently engages in a delicate equilibrium to ensure the sustainability of a country's economic expansion. Efforts are made by the central bank to regulate financial institutions in order to prevent adverse economic conditions such as recessions and economic bubbles from occurring. Furthermore, it establishes and administers policies that are in accordance with the objectives of the central government to enhance the expansion of the market.

The issuance and withdrawal of paper money falls under the purview of the central bank when it comes to currencies. An excessive quantity of currency in circulation has the potential to result in inflation, wherein the prices of goods and services within an economy experience an upward trajectory. The central bank has the capacity to mitigate inflationary pressures by regulating the quantity of currency in circulation through effective management.

Additionally, the central bank possesses the authority to establish the interest rates which banks may enact upon their borrowers. This has a direct impact on the capacity of businesses to expand. When the central bank imposes low interest rates, it incentivizes businesses to increase their borrowing in order to facilitate the expansion of their enterprises. In this particular circumstance, they engage in increased levels of borrowing owing to the prevailing low interest rates, which render the cost of borrowing funds considerably advantageous. They possess sufficient earnings to effortlessly settle both the borrowed funds and the accompanying interest charges.

When the interest rates are elevated, businesses encounter difficulty in obtaining loans due to the elevated cost of borrowing. It will necessitate a larger portion of their profits to settle both the principal sum and the associated interest of the indebtedness.

In an economic climate characterized by reduced interest rates, it is anticipated that there will be a surge in economic growth. It is highly probable that the economy will experience growth owing to an increased amount of currency in circulation. The profitability of enterprises permeates down to their employees.

Nonetheless, this particular set of economic circumstances could potentially lead to an increase in inflation. As the purchasing power of individuals expands, there is a corresponding upturn in the prices of commodities and services within the market. Should an excess of this activity persist, it is possible for the central bank to contemplate raising interest rates as a measure to moderate economic growth.

The valuation of a government-issued currency is influenced by the expertise of the central bank officials in maintaining an equilibrium between economic expansion and stability. In actuality, the values of fiat currency are determined through market activities, which are commonly referred to as the forces of supply and demand. If the economic conditions of a nation outperform those of other nations, there will be an increased inclination among foreign investors to allocate their investments in that particular country.

When such an occurrence transpires, there is a significant demand for the currency of a given nation. The prospective investors will be required to convert their currencies into the official legal tender of the country where they intend to make their investments.

When there is an increased demand for a specific fiat currency, it results in a strengthening of its value. In the event that a currency appreciates, it will necessitate a greater amount of US Dollars to procure a single unit of said currency.

Now, you may be wondering about the connection between this and cryptocurrencies. The solution can be found in one of the fundamental characteristics inherent to a cryptocurrency, wherein it functions independently of any central banking institution and its valuation remains detached from the economic performance of any nation. Consequently, the valuation of cryptocurrencies is solely contingent upon the dynamics of supply and demand within the market. Instantaneous creation or destruction of cash is not possible, thus preventing its unlimited production or elimination in situations of excess liquidity.

Over the past few years, during which multiple cryptocurrencies have been publicly traded, the absence of a governing entity has resulted in significant volatilities in the market value. Bitcoin, being the predominant cryptocurrency, frequently experiences significant value surges of a few thousand dollars per unit. When positive information regarding a cryptocurrency becomes publicly known, it elicits an augmented demand among buyers, subsequently propelling an upwards surge in the price.

The cultural phenomenon of social media

The pervasive influence of the internet and the social media ecosystem significantly shapes the dynamics of the cryptocurrency market, exerting a substantial impact on its transactions. When individuals observe acquaintances benefitting from a particular asset, they consequently develop a desire to participate in the same. Not all individuals succumb to this impulse. Nevertheless, this prevalent apprehension of missing out, commonly referred to as the Fear of Missing Out or FOMO, acts as a compelling force that propels individuals towards the realm of cryptocurrency trading.

This holds especially true for traders originating from alternative financial markets. For instance, a stock trader experiencing poor performance in the stock market may opt to reallocate a portion of their funds towards engaging in bitcoin trading. Certain individuals with substantial savings that are currently held in bank accounts may entertain the notion of allocating a portion or the entirety of these funds into the cryptocurrency market with the aim of enhancing their value. The combined efforts of individuals participating in the market contribute to the escalation of asset prices, primarily influenced by information disseminated through the media.

This holds true when individuals contemplate the prospect of making a purchase. When individuals are actively engaged in the market, they frequently contemplate the optimal timing for purchasing shares. They exhibit apprehension about prematurely withdrawing their funds due to their desire to avoid potential missed opportunities in terms of financial gains. Nonetheless, astute investors and traders recognize that every additional minute they remain engaged in the market escalates the likelihood of incurring significant losses on their earnings. In order to mitigate the risks and maximize the rewards, these individuals rely on the information disseminated through various media channels. They meticulously monitor the information pertaining to the cryptocurrency market, diligently observing any potential fluctuations in price.

The updates concerning these markets vary on a daily basis, and they are fervently sought after by both traders and individuals contemplating participation. When news of a specific story highlighting the advantages of cryptocurrencies begins to circulate, individuals commence purchasing cryptocurrencies. A modest increase in the price of bitcoin, for instance, will result in a significant amount of favorable market-related news. Consequently, this will create the perception that the market is experiencing a notable recovery, consequently encouraging individuals to resume their asset acquisition endeavors. The favorable outcomes arising from this will persistently contribute to the price system until it reaches its pinnacle.

In conventional asset markets such as the stock or commodities market, the upward trajectory of prices typically ceases once the market has attained a state of saturation. This is the occurrence in which a significant number of traders and investors have already allocated the majority of their available capital into the market. Once this juncture has been attained, short-term traders commence their implementation of profit extraction tactics. Consequently, this leads to a significant market selloff, resulting in a decline in prices.

Occasionally, it is not necessary for the point of saturation to be reached in order for an upward trend in price to come to a halt. The upward trajectory of prices may come to a sudden halt upon the dissemination of negative publicity concerning the market. During the 2018 decline in cryptocurrency value, prices underwent a significant decrease immediately following the dissemination of information regarding the enforcement of more stringent governmental regulations across various nations. Specifically, it was the economic and governmental measures implemented in the countries of East Asia and Southeast Asia that precipitated the occurrence. South

Korea, among the nations with prominent engagement in cryptocurrency trading, was included in the group of countries. The decision has been made by the South Korean government to shutter domestic cryptocurrency exchanges on the grounds of alleged involvement in illicit money laundering activities. In addition, they implemented regulations that mandated the linkage of cryptocurrency accounts to individuals' bank accounts.

Although the policies in South Korea may appear to be restrictive regarding currency trading, they pale in comparison to the stringent policies enforced by the Chinese government. China implemented a comprehensive restriction on cryptocurrency trading by effectively shutting down domestic exchanges and erecting barriers to accessing the online platforms of global exchanges.

Undoubtedly, the widespread dissemination of information regarding the implementation of policies designed to regulate, or even prohibit, cryptocurrency trading precipitated the significant market downturn observed in 2018. Considering this perspective, it is imperative that you consistently monitor the market developments when you hold cryptocurrencies for short-term durations. When encountering negative news or reports concerning the cryptocurrency with which you are engaged in trading, it is prudent to contemplate the potential magnitude of its dissemination and the consequential influence it may exert upon the market's outlook.

This leads us to the subsequent element that influences volatility:

The conduct exhibited by traders
While the book does not advocate for day trading, it is undeniable that there are individuals who have achieved longevity in this field. Skillfully employing their techniques, traders possess an exceptional ability to anticipate market trends and stay one step ahead of prevailing information and

the subsequent reactions of market participants.

The realm of cryptocurrency trading has developed into one of the most vibrant and dynamic global trading markets. The market capitalization of numerous cryptocurrencies greatly exceeds the market capitalizations of numerous companies worldwide. Within a 24-hour period, a substantial volume of bitcoins and Ether, amounting to billions of dollars, is transferred. Numerous fluctuations originate from traders seeking to capitalize on intraday market gains.

The daily fluctuations in the market are a result of the hourly transactions conducted by these traders. Despite the passing of several days subsequent to the notable downward trend observed in January and February of 2018, the market continued to demonstrate a high degree of activity. Individuals who harbored apprehension regarding further losses desired to divest themselves of their coins. Contrarily, individuals harboring an optimistic perspective during this period, diligently acquired substantial quantities of digital currencies as they permeated the market at exceptionally reduced valuations. In the subsequent months, individuals persisted in engaging in regular, active transactions of bitcoin. A portion of them consists of investors with a medium to long-term perspective who intend to remain in the market for an extended period, with the objective of capitalizing on the impending substantial price rise. The vast majority, however, consists of transient participants who engage in short-term trading and are primarily concerned with the day-to-day volatility of the market.

The actions of these individual traders will persist in causing hourly fluctuations in the prices of the predominant cryptocurrencies. You must not permit these fluctuations in prices, nonetheless, to divert your attention from your strategic objectives and aspirations. Alternatively, it is advised to prioritize the establishment of your coin portfolio.

Currently, the actions undertaken by market participants have the potential to significantly impact the valuations of cryptocurrencies. In forthcoming times, a significant appreciation can be anticipated for numerous cryptocurrencies due to increased market participation from investors. When considering the scenario where currencies of smaller market capitalization such as Ripple or Cardano display price upswings akin to bitcoin and Ethereum, their present price fluctuations might appear inconsequential. This potential escalation in prices will occur when the sentiment of the investor market transitions from pessimistic to optimistic. A pessimistic mindset does not entail a willingness to purchase cryptocurrencies. Following significant market declines such as those witnessed in 2014 and 2018, individuals tend to adopt a pessimistic outlook, characterized by a bearish sentiment.

They are averse to purchasing cryptocurrencies, consequently exerting downward pressure on prices. Once the recollection of the significant decline diminishes and optimistic reports regarding cryptocurrencies saturate the media, there arises a juncture wherein the market sentiment transitions from pessimism to optimism.

A bullish mindset pertains to the shared belief that the market is performing favorably and is anticipated to sustain this positive trajectory. This mindset is evident in the conduct of both the traders and the new participants in the market. Seasoned traders employ technical analysis of the pricing in an endeavor to anticipate the commencement of this phenomenon. Their objective is to bolster their ownership of a cryptocurrency prior to its occurrence. The aggregate cryptocurrency purchases made by the group, accompanied by the buying activities of the recent entrants in the market, propel the price to unprecedented heights.

The rate of inflation in the country from which your operational fiat currency originates.

The purchasing power of a country's fiat currency is influenced by the inflation rates experienced within that nation. In the event that the United States, for instance, encounters a significant inflationary trend, it will lead to a depreciation of the US dollar. In the event of a depreciation in the value of the US dollar, a greater amount of it would be required to purchase cryptocurrencies. Regrettably, the volatility of the US dollar or any other fiat currency is also a matter of concern. While it may not possess the same level of volatility as cryptocurrencies, it has the potential to undergo sufficient daily fluctuations that can impact the exchange rate of cryptocurrency to fiat currency.

To safeguard your investment portfolio against the adverse impact of this factor, it is advisable to refrain from purchasing cryptocurrency during periods characterized by high inflation rates. In the current circumstances, it will be necessary for you to allocate a greater portion of your fiat currency towards the purchase of cryptocurrency. It is advisable to exercise patience and wait for a favorable appreciation of your currency's value before initiating the purchase of cryptocurrencies.

It is furthermore recommended to refrain from engaging in conversions between traditional currencies in order to conduct transactions within the cryptocurrency market. Let's say your credit card is in Euro. It is advisable to exclusively engage with exchanges that employ the Euro as their primary operational currency. There is no necessity for you to convert your Euros into US Dollars. Engaging in the interchange of two standard currencies exposes your investment capital to supplementary risks.

Various Categories Of Cryptocurrencies

When the term cryptocurrency is brought up, the majority of individuals immediately associate it with Bitcoin. Cryptocurrency serves as an alternative appellation for Bitcoin, according to some individuals. This is primarily due to the fact that Bitcoin served as the pioneer and frontrunner in a burgeoning wave of cryptocurrencies that operate on a decentralized peer-to-peer network. Nevertheless, cryptocurrencies encompass a broader spectrum beyond the realm of Bitcoin. To date, there exists a plethora of more than 1500 distinct classifications of cryptocurrencies. Numerous additions are being made to the world on a daily basis. Bitcoin's establishment as the foremost player in the realm of cryptographic currencies has led to the categorization of other cryptocurrencies as 'altcoins,' denoting their nature as alternative options to

Bitcoin. The majority of these alternative cryptocurrencies were influenced by Bitcoin. Numerous individuals employ a modified iteration of the Bitcoin protocol, incorporating certain alterations to align with their fundamental aim. Nevertheless, it should be noted that not all alternative coins are simply derivations or modifications of Bitcoin. Certain developers have constructed their alternative cryptocurrencies entirely from the ground up, employing a unique underlying framework of their own design.

Notwithstanding the presence of myriad cryptocurrencies, only a select few possess any degree of significance. Among them, an even smaller fraction has succeeded in attaining a market capitalization exceeding $1 million. In the subsequent section, an examination will be conducted on several significant cryptocurrencies.

Bitcoin (BTC)

This cryptocurrency represents a groundbreaking achievement as the foremost and widely recognized digital currency in the modern era. Despite the limited comprehension that most individuals may possess on the subject, Bitcoin has managed to achieve widespread recognition among nearly all segments of society. Bitcoin is an decentralized electronic payment system that enables direct transactions between users, eliminating the need for any intermediary involvement and allowing for immediate transaction processing. Bitcoin made its inaugural entry into the global realm in October 2008 when a purported individual named Satoshi Nakamoto released a detailed document elucidating the underlying structure and operational mechanism of this digital currency. In the month of January 2009, Nakamoto successfully engaged in the process of mining the inaugural Bitcoin Block, commonly known as the Genesis block, thereby initiating the existence of the initial units of the digital currency, known as Bitcoins. Nakamoto's primary intention in creating Bitcoin was to facilitate the decentralized control of currency, shifting it away from centralized entities such as banks and governments. This parallel can be drawn with the advent of the internet, which decentralized and democratized access to information, placing power in the hands of the general public.

Freshly minted Bitcoins are generated as a form of incentive for engaging in the mining process, which serves as the essential mechanism to sustain the operational integrity of the Bitcoin protocol. The Bitcoin protocol is structured to maintain the production rate of new Bitcoins at a consistent average level. As additional computational resources are allocated towards Bitcoin mining, the complexity of the mining process increases. When a portion of the network's processing power is allocated elsewhere, it leads to a decrease in the mining difficulty for generating new Bitcoins. The governing guidelines were established with a predetermined threshold of 21 million Bitcoins, beyond which the supply of Bitcoins will cease to expand.

Bitcoin was created with the intention of serving as a means of conducting financial transactions. Consequently, individuals have the opportunity to utilize Bitcoin as a medium of exchange for the acquisition of various goods and services, whether through online platforms or in physical establishments. At present, a significant number of businesses have incorporated Bitcoin as a form of payment, totaling in the hundreds of thousands. In addition to utilizing Bitcoin for the purchase of goods and services, Bitcoin can also be exchanged for alternative currencies or retained as an investment. The act of regarding Bitcoin as a form of investment has gained significant traction in 2017, witnessing a considerable surge in value from under

$1000 at the commencement of the year to nearly $20,000 by the conclusion of the same year.

Bitcoin has the capacity to be subdivided into smaller units, namely millibitcoins, microbitcoins, and satoshis. The Satoshi (0.00000001) is acknowledged as the most diminutive denomination of Bitcoin, paying homage to the enigmatic originator of the cryptocurrency. Being the pioneering cryptocurrency, Bitcoin is readily accessible and enjoys extensive adoption. Bitcoin is additionally characterized by its immense size, with a market value surpassing $300 billion, thereby surpassing the collective market capitalization of all alternative cryptocurrencies included in this compilation.

Ethereum (ETH)

Bitcoin holds the position of utmost popularity and market capitalization, with Ethereum securing the second spot. Similar to Bitcoin, Ethereum is a form of cryptocurrency that operates on an open source and decentralized platform, utilizing blockchain technology. In contrast to Bitcoin, Ethereum does not function as a payment platform. Conversely, it serves as a platform in which developers can construct and implement diverse types of decentralized applications based on blockchain technology, commonly known as DApps. The cryptographic units or currency of the Ethereum protocol are commonly referred to as Ether. One of the most prominent characteristics of Ethereum is its utilization of "smart contracts", programming code that enables the secure and seamless transfer of value, entirely safeguarded against fraudulent activities or external interference. This denotes that in addition to monetary exchanges, the Ethereum platform enables the utilization of smart contracts for the transfer of various assets, including but not limited to shares, land titles, and car ownership. Ethereum was brought into existence and subsequently launched in the year 2015 by Vitalik Buterin, an accomplished programmer of Russian and Canadian descent, who was at the time in his youth.

In the grand scheme of things, Ethereum exhibits significantly greater potential in comparison to Bitcoin. Despite both utilizing blockchain technology, the two rival cryptocurrencies exhibit significant disparities with regards to their goals and capabilities. Bitcoin functions exclusively as a payment system, representing solely one aspect of the wider range of applications possible with blockchain technology. Rather than directing attention solely towards a singular utility like Bitcoin, Ethereum provides a platform for developers to construct a myriad of decentralized applications. This implies that Ethereum possesses the potential to completely transform all centralized services and sectors. Similar to Bitcoin, the value of

Ethereum has experienced an extraordinary increase in 2017. The value of a single unit of Ether experienced a significant increase from under $10 at the start of the year to surpassing $750 by the conclusion of the year. Currently, the market capitalization of Ethereum stands at approximately $83 billion.

Presently, there exist two coexisting Ethereum blockchains, namely Ethereum (ETH) and Ethereum Classic (ETC). The introduction of Ethereum Classic occurred subsequent to a division that ensued in the wake of the security breach of the DAO project, which was built on the Ethereum platform, in September 2016, resulting in the theft of approximately $50 million worth of Ether.

Litecoin (LTC)

Litecoin is recognized as one of the pioneering cryptocurrencies that arose in the wake of Bitcoin's emergence. Dissatisfied with the protracted delays associated with Bitcoin transactions, Charles Lee, a software engineer employed by Google, took it upon himself to develop an independent cryptocurrency as an alternative to Bitcoin. This cryptocurrency, known as Litecoin, was introduced to the public in 2011. Lee's intention in launching Litecoin was to implement incremental yet impactful modifications that would enhance the efficacy of Bitcoin and other cryptocurrencies that depended on the proof of work (POW) verification mechanism.

Lee's notable modification entailed the alteration of the cryptographic hash function employed within Litecoin. In contrast to Bitcoin's utilization of the SHA256 hash function, Lee implemented the 'scrypt' algorithm in Litecoin. The transition to employing the 'scrypt' algorithm enabled Litecoin to expedite the processing and verification of transactions. The verification process of

Litecoin transactions typically concludes within approximately two minutes, whereas Bitcoin transactions may necessitate up to 10 minutes for confirmation. One additional benefit of utilizing the 'scrypt' algorithm is that it facilitated coin mining for users with consumer-grade CPUs, in contrast to Bitcoin, which mandates that miners possess specialized mining CPUs.

Lee upheld the inherent scarcity that is intrinsic to Bitcoin. Nevertheless, it is worth noting that Litecoin is constrained by a maximum supply of 84 million coins, in contrast to Bitcoin's limit of 21 million. Through this action, Lee enhanced the liquidity of Litecoin by increasing the supply of available coins, thus mitigating the prevalent phenomenon of hoarding observed among Bitcoin investors. An additional significant distinction between Litecoin and Bitcoin lies in the utilization of a marginally altered mining protocol by Litecoin. This protocol enables a more equitable allocation of the mined coins.

Additionally, Litecoin facilitates expeditious testing and integration of novel technological advancements. As an example, Litecoin was an early adopter and successfully deployed SegWit (Segregated Witness) technology long before Bitcoin. Overall, Litecoin possesses a robust nature as a noteworthy digital currency, characterized by its favorable standing and sound economic framework. At present, Litecoin's market capitalization stands at approximately $19 billion.

IOTA (IOT)

The creators of IOTA constructed it with the purpose of establishing it as the fundamental infrastructure for the Internet of Things (IOT). The term 'Internet of Things' pertains to the interconnected network of everyday physical objects that are equipped with embedded sensors to gather and transmit data via the internet. The realm of Internet of Things (IOT) encompasses a wide array of elements, ranging from automobiles and computers equipped with internet connectivity to kitchen appliances, microchips, home automation systems, and devices implemented in healthcare facilities, among other examples. IOTA aspires to realize its objective of serving as the fundamental framework for the Internet of Things, positioning itself as the encompassing ledger for all interconnected devices and systems.

In addition to serving as the fundamental infrastructure of the Internet of Things, IOTA was crafted with the purpose of addressing various obstacles encountered by Bitcoin. These include concerns related to scalability, speed, and transaction fees. IOTA encompasses a distinguishing factor that sets it apart from other cryptocurrencies, such as Bitcoin. While Bitcoin and the majority of other cryptocurrencies are founded on blockchain technology, IOTA is established on a distinct mechanism called the 'Tangle'. The Tangle refers to a Directed Acyclic Graph (DAG), an alternative form of distributed ledger that operates on a distinct protocol separate from the conventional blockchain protocol.

In the context of blockchain-based digital currencies, it is imperative that a transaction undergoes verification by the interconnected network of computers prior to its finalization. Verification is not dependent on the network when utilizing the Tangle. On the contrary, the Tangle utilizes a system wherein the sender is mandated to undertake a proof of work prior to executing their transaction. Through this action, the sender provides their consent to two transactions, effectively merging the transaction with its corresponding validation process. As it falls within the domain of the sender to furnish the evidence of work, the involvement of miners becomes superfluous.

This has two benefits. Initially, through the removal of miners, the Tangle ensures complete decentralization of IOTA. Rather than having players who have an impact on the network without actively utilizing it, the IOTA network is exclusively upheld by the "users" who actively engage in transactions. Furthermore, the implementation of requiring the sender to endorse two transactions prior to executing their own transaction effectively enhances the swiftness of the IOTA protocol. Furthermore, it implies that an augmentation in the user count results in expedited validation speed. This diverges from the typical occurrences observed with other cryptocurrencies such as Bitcoin, wherein the validation time is impeded by a growing user base. Due to the absence of miners, users are exempted from any obligation to contribute fees for network maintenance as well. In 2017, IOTA experienced favorable growth, culminating in a market capitalization of $11 billion at the close of the year.

Ripple (XRP)

Ripple is a cutting-edge platform crafted with the purpose of facilitating instantaneous worldwide settlements, while also serving as a robust network for currency exchange and remittance. The primary purpose of Ripple tokens does not entail their utilization as a medium of exchange for goods and services. On the contrary, the network was structured with the primary aim of facilitating immediate conversions between diverse fiat currencies, all the while circumventing the need for a central exchange. After its introduction in 2012, several financial institutions have embraced Ripple as a financially efficient solution for facilitating cross-border transactions.

In contrast to numerous cryptocurrencies present, Ripple was not developed as a derivative or alternative form of Bitcoin. On the contrary, the developers constructed it entirely from the ground up and integrated significant alterations into its framework. In contrast to the majority of cryptocurrencies that employ proof of stake or proof of work mechanisms for transaction verification, Ripple utilizes a distinct consensus system wherein the computers within the network continuously monitor alterations. After a consensus is reached among the majority of the computers in the network, the transaction is incorporated into the public ledger. The consensus system presents several advantages in comparison to the proof of work or proof of stake systems. Transactions that undergo verification within the consensus system are promptly validated and entail reduced processing requirements. Although hackers may appear capable of compromising the consensus system, its design ensures that the network rejects any inaccurate outcomes.

Given that the objective of the Ripple network is to facilitate cross-currency conversions, Ripples have the capability to be traded for an extensive selection of fiat currencies as well as alternative cryptocurrencies. Additionally, select establishments provide the option for customers to convert Ripples into air miles and loyalty points. In contrast to altcoins such as Ether and Litecoin, which are traded on cryptocurrency exchanges, the acquisition of Ripple requires the utilization of Gateways. The functionality of the Gateways is akin to that of PayPal. Presently, the market capitalization of Ripple stands at approximately $30 billion.

Dash (Dash)

Dash is a digital currency which can be credited to the ingenuity of Evan Duffield and Kyle Hagan. Originally referred to as Darkcoin, it was initially introduced in 2014. Following one year of establishment, the organization underwent a rebranding process resulting in the adoption of the name "Dash," derived from the term "Digital Cash." Kyle and Evan aspired to establish a highly discreet and anonymous cryptocurrency through the development of Dash. The majority of cryptocurrencies do not possess complete anonymity. Although addresses are not associated with personally identifiable information, the network retains information regarding the quantity of coins held in each address, and the movement of coins between addresses can be monitored by anyone. This enables individuals to ascertain the identities of users who fail to employ measures to safeguard their anonymity. In order to maintain user anonymity, Dash utilizes a decentralized mastercode network, rendering Dash transactions exceedingly arduous to trace.

The considerable degree of anonymization provided by Dash is facilitated by a mechanism referred to as Darksend. Through the utilization of this system, designated computers referred to as mastercodes gather multiple transactions and carry out their execution simultaneously, thereby ensuring the invisibility of the transactions. It becomes infeasible to ascertain the origin and destination of the coins. In order to further enhance the level of anonymity in your transactions, you may opt to engage the mastercodes to facilitate multiple sequential rounds of transaction mixing prior to finalizing the transaction. In order to preserve this level of anonymity, public access to the Dash ledger is restricted. The considerable level of obscurity has also hindered widespread adoption among businesses.

Another notable characteristic that sets Dash apart is its unique hashing algorithm. Rather than employing the SHA256 or scrypt hash functions, Dash cryptocurrency utilizes an exclusive X11 hash, enabling individuals with standard

CPUs to engage in mining Dash coins due to its reduced processing power requirements. Additional noteworthy benefits of Dash include its rapid verification of transactions, typically taking around 4 seconds, as well as its cost-effective transaction fees. Nevertheless, it is anticipated that the charges will increase as the network attracts a larger number of participants. Additionally, Dash employs a voting system to facilitate the swift execution of critical modifications. With a market capitalization of approximately $9 billion, Dash exhibits a notably elevated price per unit compared to other alternative cryptocurrencies.

Monero (XMR)

Monero is an additional form of digital currency that shares a similar emphasis on maintaining privacy and ensuring anonymity, akin to Dash. Monero was initiated in 2014 by a group of seven programmers, of whom five made the conscious decision to maintain their anonymity. Owing to its anonymity attributes, it swiftly garnered favor among cryptocurrency enthusiasts. Similar to the majority of other cryptocurrencies, Monero is completely based on open source software. The progression of the platform is shaped by contributions from the community and generous financial support. Monero is derived from a highly robust cryptographic protocol called 'CryptoNote'. Furthermore, it employs a distinctive cryptographic hash function referred to as 'CryptoNight'. In order to uphold the utmost level of anonymity and privacy, Monero employs the technique of 'ring signatures'. This methodology represents a digitized counterpart of group signatures. Every transaction conducted on the Monero network is enveloped by a set of cryptographic signatures. In this manner, it becomes exceedingly challenging to identify the precise originator or recipient of the transaction. Even in the presence of an individual's wallet address, the observation of the precise quantity of coins within the wallet or the monitoring of the corresponding expenditure locations remains unattainable. Consequently, Monero coins are inherently resistant to becoming tarnished due to preceding questionable transactions.

Monero transactions undergo verification utilizing the identical proof of work mechanism employed by Bitcoin. Nevertheless, a significant distinction can be observed between Bitcoin and Monero, whereby Bitcoin imposes a restriction of 2MB on block sizes, whereas Monero does not enact any limitation on block sizes. The absence of restricted block sizes poses a potential threat where malevolent miners could exploit excessively enormous blocks to congest the system. In order to prevent such occurrences, the system incorporates an inherent penalty system for block rewards.

Consequently, should a miner successfully extract a new block surpassing the median size determined by the previous 100 blocks, their corresponding block reward shall be proportionally diminished in relation to the extent to which the new block surpasses said median size. The present market capitalization of Monero stands at $5 billion.

Neo (NEO)

Neo represents a Chinese digital currency that came into existence courtesy of the collaborative efforts of Erik Zhang and Da Hongfei. Neo has been developed as an intelligent economic infrastructure, sharing similarities with Ethereum. It has also been denoted as the 'Ethereum of China'. Originally introduced as Antshares, Neo made its initial entry into the market. In the month of August in the year 2017, a rebranding initiative was undertaken which led to the establishment of the NEO Smart Contract Economy. The objective of NEO closely aligns with that of Ethereum. NEO offers a platform wherein developers are able to create decentralized applications and implement smart contracts. In contrast to Ethereum, which exclusively supports its Solidity programming language, NEO provides compatibility with widely-used programming languages like C#, Python, and Java.

A fundamental divergence between NEO and Ethereum can be observed in the verification mechanisms employed by these platforms. While Ethereum employs a hybrid validation mechanism comprising proof of stake and proof of work, NEO operates on a consensus protocol known as Delegated Byzantine Fault Tolerance (dBFT). In this particular system, rather than enlisting the participation of all computers, designated nodes assume the responsibility of being bookkeepers. It is the responsibility of these bookkeepers to authenticate blocks prior to their inclusion in the blockchain. If a majority of at least two-thirds of the computers within the network concur with the bookkeeper's rendition, consensus is attained, subsequently validating the new block and appending it to the blockchain. In the event that a consensus cannot be reached, an alternative bookkeeper is summoned and the entire process is reiterated.

Given that consensus under the dBFT system must only be reached by a subset of the network, this particular system necessitates a lower utilization of processing power and grants the network the ability to effectively manage a greater influx of transactions. NEO asserts its capacity to process more than 1000 transactions per second, while Ethereum's capabilities are limited to 15 transactions per second. The dBFT system additionally eradicates the potential occurrence of a hard fork, rendering NEO an excellent choice for the digitization of tangible financial assets. The present valuation of NEO stands at approximately $4 billion in market capitalization.

OmiseGO (OMG)

OmiseGO has garnered significant attention among aficionados of cryptocurrencies in recent times. Having been initiated in the year of 2013, this project is both intriguing and exceedingly ambitious in its objective of utilizing Ethereum's financial technology to provide banking services to those already affiliated with traditional banking systems. Presently, OmiseGO is constructed upon the Ethereum platform as an ERC20 token, however, it is anticipated to subsequently deploy its self-governing blockchain. OmiseGO aspires to establish itself as the foremost peer-to-peer cryptocurrency exchange platform. OmiseGO is not merely classified as an altcoin; it is substantively designed as a comprehensive financial platform that seeks to revolutionize and disrupt the prevailing financial sector.

OmiseGO endeavors to address a predicament that has eluded the resolution of the majority of cryptocurrency exchanges. In order to acquire a cryptocurrency through the majority of cryptocurrency exchanges, it is necessary to initiate the transaction with a fiat currency. In order to engage in altcoin conversion, it is necessary to convert the altcoins into fiat currency or Bitcoin and subsequently reconvert the fiat/Bitcoin into the desired altcoins. During the entirety of this process, the exchange imposes charges for every transaction. Consequently, you will incur charges for the conversion of the initial altcoins into fiat/Bitcoin, and once more for the conversion of the fiat/Bitcoin into the subsequent altcoins.

OmiseGO aims to address this issue through the integration of all prevailing cryptocurrency wallets with a centralized OmiseGO blockchain. In this manner, users are able to conveniently trade alternative cryptocurrencies for one another without the need to convert them into traditional currency or Bitcoin. This implies that, rather than incurring numerous charges, users will be subjected to a singular minimal fee.

OmiseGO also endeavors to facilitate decentralization within cryptocurrency exchanges. Presently, the majority of exchanges function as centralized entities. The company's servers store databases containing records of all transactions, as well as data pertaining to various users. OmiseGO seeks to achieve the decentralization of exchange functionality through the establishment of a system wherein the storage of all transaction information and user data is conducted on the blockchain. In this manner, the security of the data is enhanced as it would necessitate a hacker to execute a 51% attack, gaining dominance over a majority (51%) of the computers within the network, in order to undermine the integrity of the blockchain. Achieving such a feat is highly improbable in practice. Presently, OmiseGO exhibits a market capitalization hovering around the $1 billion mark.

NEM (XEM)

NEM is an innovative digital currency that was introduced in March 2015. In contrast to numerous other cryptocurrencies that emerged as derivatives of existing endeavors, NEM was meticulously developed from scratch, featuring its distinctive source code. NEM's nomenclature can be traced back to the New Economic Movement, the collective responsible for the inception of this digital currency. NEM is specifically engineered as a blockchain technology adaptable to accommodate diverse business requirements. The fundamental essence of NEM's protocol resides in the 'Smart Asset System.'

Given its inherent customizability, NEM possesses boundless potential to accommodate a diverse range of applications. It finds utility as a primary ledger within the banking industry, serving as a mechanism for maintaining trustworthy records. Additionally, it enables the implementation of a blockchain-powered voting framework, functions as an intermediary for escrow services, facilitates the allocation of loyalty program points, drives crowd funding initiatives, and provides a platform for managing stock ownership, among other applications. This exemplifies the considerable potential inherent in NEM.

In contrast to the majority of cryptocurrency platforms, NEM offers a messaging platform. Additionally, it possesses a system for granting rewards and is capable of facilitating multisignature transactions. One of the principal distinctions distinguishing NEM from other cryptocurrencies lies in its authentication process. Rather than employing proof of work or proof of stake, NEM utilizes a distinct proof of importance mechanism, whereby opportunities for block computation are allocated according to a user's contribution to the advancement and dissemination of the platform. Individuals who demonstrate a significant level of contribution are granted additional opportunities as a form of recognition. This facilitates equitable distribution of mining opportunities among users.

The NEM network exhibits high speed, characterized by a transaction verification delay of approximately one minute. This signifies that NEM can be depended upon for facilitating immediate international financial transfers. The utilization of the proof of importance system eliminates the necessity for users to possess costly hardware in order to engage in NEM coin mining. The current valuation of NEM's market capitalization amounts to approximately $8 billion.

www.ingramcontent.com/pod-product-compliance
Lightning Source LLC
Chambersburg PA
CBHW050235120526
44590CB00016B/2103